Vertical Worship
What is it and how do I do it?

Angela D. Brown

Copyright © 2012 Angela D. Brown
4th Edition

Published by
BUT GOD! Publishings
https://butgod.wixsite.com/butgodpublishings

All rights reserved. No part of this publication may be reproduced, stored in a retrieval system or transmitted in any form by any means, electronic, mechanical, photocopy, recording or otherwise, without the prior permission of the publisher.
For information contact:
The Vertical Print Shop
1195 St. Matthews Road #190
Orangeburg, SC 29115

All scripture quotations unless otherwise indicated are taken from the Holy Bible King James Version

Scripture quotations marked from NKJV are taken from the New King James Version copyrighted © 1982 by Thomas Nelson Inc. Used by permission. All rights reserved.

Scripture quotations marked NIV are from the International Bible Society copyrighted in June 1978. Published by Broadman & Holman

Scripture quotations marked HCSB have been taken from the Holman Christian Standard Bible ® Copyright © 1999, 2000, 2002, 2003, 2009 by Holman Bible Publishers. Used by Permission Holman Christian Standard Bible ® Holman CSB ®

Dedication

This book is dedicated to my
Lord and Savior Jesus Christ
who first taught me how to
worship vertically

*In loving memory of my mother, Betty J. Brown —
Mom, now you are worshipping before the throne
without earthly distractions*

Table of Contents

Introduction	1
What is Vertical Worship?	3
What is the purpose?	7
Why Vertical Worship?	9
How do we Worship Vertically?	11
1) Knowing God	11
2) Dying To Self	14
3) Practicing His Presence	17
4) Acknowledging His Deity	21
5) Tell Him you love Him often	23
6) Develop a lasting friendship with Him	25
7) Sing love songs to Him	27
8) Acknowledge Personage of the Holy Spirit	29
The Benefits of Vertical Worship	31
The Vertical Worshipper	33
My Paradigm Shift	34
Living for the Well Done	36
The Heart Cry of Vertical Worship	38
My Worship Is Vertical!	39
A Word on Fasting	39
My Declarations	41
In Summary	42
The Surrendered Life	43

A Personal Conviction Disclaimer

I have a personal reverence for the Lord, which will stand out in this book. Out of profound respect, I capitalize the pronouns when referring to God, Jesus or the Holy Spirit (even in scriptural reference). So though it may be grammatically incorrect, you will see capitalization of the following words throughout my writings: He, Him, His, My, Mine, You, and Yours.

INTRODUCTION

"Seek those things which are above where Christ is sitting at the right-hand side of God." Colossians 3:1

In 2008, I was preparing to host my 7th Annual International Creative Arts Conference in Austin, Texas. As I was seeking the Lord for the topic of the conference, He gave me these two words: VERTICAL WORSHIP. I thought to myself, "That's a good topic. As creative artists, we should direct our worship vertically toward the Lord." It was a catchy phrase, and I thought everyone would be excited about the new theme. Then the Lord gave me a vision for the logo. He showed me the words Vertical Worship on a cross. The word "Vertical" was to be on the upward beam with an arrow tip, representing our (mankind) position as we reach out to God. The word "Worship" was to be on the horizontal beam, representing God's outreach to the world. Next, He gave me the scriptural reference Colossians 3:1-4, which I had the artist place in the arrow tip of the cross. Below is the entire passage: *"1 If ye then be risen with Christ, seek those things which are above, where Christ sitteth on the right hand of God. 2 Set your affection on things above, not on things on the earth. 3 For ye are dead, and your life is hid with Christ in God. 4 When Christ, who is our life, shall appear, then shall ye also appear with Him in glory."* The Vertical Worship concept was born: before we can minister to the world horizontally, we must first minister to the Lord vertically.

Once we had the logo, we had conference T-shirts and bags made with the Vertical Worship logo printed on them. Now we were ready! I envisioned we would all get caught up in worship and the conference would end in a blaze of glory. However, when I posed the question to the registrants during our first general session, *"What do you think Vertical Worship means?"* I was met with blank stares and no response. I was shocked! Surely the words speak for themselves. After all, this is what we do every Sunday and what we should do every day during our personal devotional time with the Lord. I gave them an explanation of the theme and we continued with the conference, which turned out to be a success, but I had no idea this was just a precursor for what the Lord really wanted me to do.

Two years later, in 2010, I could not shake the concept of Vertical Worship. Once again, the Lord gave me "Let's Go Vertical" as the conference theme and once again, the conference was a success, yet many still did not get the full revelation.

While preparing our 2012 conference, I sought the Lord and asked Him what He would have me do with this burden He had given me concerning worship. Worshipping God is not a new concept. Worship leaders have been leading us in the praise & worship portion of our services for decades, directing our focus to the Lord. Worshipping God in our personal lives is required to maintain a healthy relationship with the Lord. So why was He giving me such a burden? I still didn't quite understand it, but a few years ago I began to feel sorrow in my heart concerning the lackadaisical attitude that we have taken when it comes to worshipping God. It's almost like we think we are doing Him a favor by showing up on Sundays!

Before I go any further, I want to stop here and share my heart with you concerning the purpose of this book. Like the beams on the cross go both ways, horizontally and vertically, we as human beings are very relational. We need to communicate with each other in order to survive, therefore we must work on our horizontal relationships. However, we who use the name of Christ must also maintain a relationship with our God, and we do that through the spirit, which is a vertical relationship. Unfortunately, we often spend more time on our horizontal relationships than the vertical one, and this can make us more people-centered than Christ-centered. However, on the flip side, there are those who put more emphasis on the vertical than the horizontal and they can become so heavenly minded that they do no earthly good. We need balance. The bottom line is, we need to work on our relationship with mankind while simultaneously working on our relationship with God. While I do not want to negate this very important aspect of existence, the main purpose for this book is to point the reader vertically.

Our personal relationship with God is crucial to the success of any other relationship we have here on earth. Therefore, while we recognize the importance of the horizontal relationship with mankind, our unique calling is to put emphasis on the vertical relationship with the Lord.

Chapter One

What is Vertical Worship?

[Vertical Worship is having a single focus on the Lord – Tunnel Vision]

"But the hour cometh, and now is, when the true worshippers shall worship the Father in spirit and in truth: for the Father seeketh such to worship Him."
John 4:23

We are truly in the last days, for so many of the signs are very clear. *"...Men have become lovers of their own selves, covetous, boasters, proud, blasphemers, disobedient to parents, unthankful, unholy ...Traitors, heady, high-minded, lovers of pleasures more than lovers of God."* II Tim 3:2, 4 (KJV) This is the expected behavior of the world because their minds have not yet been regenerated, but what saddens my heart is that these are becoming the characteristics of the Body of Christ as well. What stands out the most to me in this scripture is when it says men have become *"...lovers of pleasures more than lovers of God."* (v4) Oh how this must hurt the heart of God! I'm not saying that we cannot enjoy life. But when we allow the cares and pleasures of this world to consume us more than our relationship with God, our priorities are out of order. God wants us to have balance. He wants us to have life and that more abundantly. He wishes above all that we prosper and be in good health as our souls prosper, but not at the expense of our personal relationship with Him.

VERTICAL WORSHIP. What does that mean? Do I stand upright with uplifted hands and direct my gaze to heaven? Or do I prostrate myself on my face before the Lord God Almighty, or do I sit silently in His Presence as I ponder on His goodness and mercies toward me? All these attitudes of worship are correct. I believe that what the Lord is, and has always been, looking for are true worshippers, as declared in John 4:23.

According to Merriam's Webster Dictionary and Dictionary.com, the word **vertical** means "rising perpendicularly from a level surface, upright, erect, standing." The word **worship** means "adoration, homage, loving devotion, respect, and reverence paid to a divine being."

Combine them together and **Vertical Worship** means to respect and revere a divine being uprightly. It means directing our focus upward to God and fixing our eyes on Him and Him alone. Vertical Worship has God as its primary focus. All of our praise adoration, respect, devotion, and attention are aimed directly at Him. We look **vertically** because our God dwells in heavenly places and heaven is in the upward direction. We **worship** because He is worthy of our adoration.

Let's look a little deeper at the meaning of the word worship. The Greek word "**proskuneo**" means to kiss the master's hand, to fawn or crouch, to prostate oneself in homage, to revere, to adore, to worship. The Hebrew word "**barak**" means to kneel or bow, to give reverence to God as an act of adoration. It implies a continual conscious giving place to God, to be attuned to Him and His presence. Can you imagine just laying out before the Lord face down, prostrate in His Presence? That is the ultimate in total submission.

Proskuneo & *barak* epitomize what true worship is. Worship is not just something we do haphazardly. Worship is intentional. Worship is a very deliberate act. Worship is a very selfless act. In order to partake in true worship, we must first have a relationship with God. True worship cannot be drummed up or performed. True worship is a matter of the heart. It is private. It is a very personal affair.

Let's look at Colossians 3:1-4, quoted earlier, *"**1** If ye then be risen with Christ, seek those things which are above, where Christ sitteth on the right hand of God. **2** Set your affection on things above, not on things on the earth. **3** For ye are dead, and your life is hid with Christ in God. **4** When Christ, who is our life, shall appear, then shall ye also appear with Him in glory."* How does this portion of scripture pertain to Vertical Worship? The first verse **tells us who** should partake in Vertical Worship. We can tell that Paul is addressing Christians, *"If ye then be risen with Christ…"* In other words, if you name the name of Christ, if you say that Christ is your Savior, *"then seek those things which are above where Christ sits on the right hand of God."* Seek those things where Christ abides. And where does Christ live? He lives in heaven. And what are those "things" which are "above" where Christ is in heaven? What kind of "things" are going on in Heaven?

Merriam-Webster defines **"things"** as *possessions, whatever may be possessed or owned. Anything that is or may be an object of thought.*

What type of "things" would Christ possess or own? Let's take a look:
1. Eternal life
2. Peace
3. Obedience to the Father
4. Divine healing
5. Forgiveness of sins
6. Right relationship with the Father

Just to name a few. Christ is the embodiment of the scriptures. There is so much to seek after! We will spend a lifetime seeking after all the "things" Christ seeks after.

The second verse **shows us how** to partake in Vertical Worship: *"Set your affection on things above, not on things on the earth."* Set your devotion, your fond attachment, your love on things pertaining to the Kingdom of God.

Philippians 3:20 states, *"For our citizenship is in heaven, from which we also eagerly wait for the Savior, the Lord Jesus Christ. Who will transform our lowly body that it may be conformed to His glorious body, according to the working by which He is able, even to subdue all things to Himself."* (NKJV) This scripture clearly explains that our citizenship is in heaven! We are just passing through here on earth. Every kingdom has a king, and every king has a throne. Heaven is our Kingdom and Jesus is our King and He is seated at the right hand of God the Father on the throne. Therefore, we need to direct our worship to where our King is dwelling!

Paul is trying to help us change our mindsets to stop focusing on the temporal things here on earth and be more God-conscientious and focus on the everlasting things in Heaven. And what does Heaven represent? (Revelations 21:4)
1. God's residence, where His Presence lights up the place
2. Everlasting joy and peace
3. No more pain and tears
4. A place of non-stop worship

Verse three shows **the purpose** of Vertical Worship: *"For ye are dead, and your life is hid with Christ in God."* You are a walking dead man. Because you have accepted Christ and are raised together with Him, you are now dead to sin and alive to Christ. The scripture says that your life is now hidden in Christ, which means that you are so submerged in Christ that people no longer see you, but only Christ exemplified through your lifestyle. Your identity is totally in Christ. It's no longer about you—IT'S ALL ABOUT HIM. He takes preeminence in your life. Totally surrendered. A totally surrendered life has no agenda. A totally surrendered life has no impure motives. A totally surrendered life wants to please God.

Lastly, verse four shows **the results** of Vertical Worship: *"When Christ, who is our life, shall appear, then shall ye also appear with Him in glory."* This is God's promise of eternal life. If we who confess that Jesus Christ is our personal Savior will seek with our whole hearts for those things that give Him pleasure from above, then our lives will be hidden in Him and when He appears in glory, we will be right there with Him. Hallelujah!

In summary, Vertical Worship is setting our affection, our devotion to things above, focusing on things pertaining to the Kingdom of God. Vertical Worship is blocking out the world and focusing all our attention on God. Vertical Worship is going into the Lord's presence with no hidden agenda. Vertical Worship is going pass the exterior of worship and going into a deeper intimacy with God, seeking the deeper truths of God. Vertical Worshippers are those who worship Him with reckless abandonment, unashamedly, purely, and without self-motive.

Vertical Worship, as revealed to me, is simply this: before we can effectively minister, serve, impart, or impact the world (believers and non-believers) horizontally, we must first align ourselves with the Lord vertically.

Chapter Two

WHAT IS THE PURPOSE?
[Vertical Worship is Intentional]

"That I may know Him and the power of His resurrection, and the fellowship of His sufferings, being conformed to His death,"
Philippians 3:10

According to Matthew 24:10-12, *"And then many will be offended, will betray one another, and will hate one another. Then many false prophets will rise up and deceive many. And because lawlessness will abound, the love of many will grow cold."* This passage indicates the plight of mankind today. Those who once loved the Lord and served Him unconditionally now find themselves going to church as a Sunday morning ritual rather than an opportunity to come and pay homage to the King of Kings and Lord of Lords. The passion that they once had for the Lord is literally gone.

The real question is, why should we worship God at all? The short answer is to stay connected with our heavenly Father. The biblical answer is that it brings pleasure to God: *"The **Lord** is pleased with those who **worship** Him and trust His love."* (Psalm 147:11)

Wycliffe's Bible Encyclopedia has one of the best definitions I've seen regarding the purpose of worship:
"The purpose of worship is to establish or to give expression to a relationship between creature and Deity. Pure worship expresses adoration without making petition."

So, what is the purpose of Vertical Worship? Aren't we all called to worship vertically? God reigns in Heavenly places, therefore our worship has no other direction except up. Right? But you would be surprised how many Christians are not focused **vertically**. We are focused on our jobs, circumstances, and relationships—not that these things are not important, or do not deserve our undivided attention, but neither should they CONSUME US. Our priorities must be in order: **Christ first** and everything else second.

The main purpose for Vertical Worship is to focus our hearts on the Lord and to come to know Him in a more intimate and personal relationship. To not only love Him for what He has done, but fall madly in love with Him for who He is. Besides the mandate God sets out in John 4:24,"...*and those who worship Him* **must worship** *in spirit and truth*", real worship is birthed out of a real relationship with God. It's not a burden, it's not a chore, and it's not even a command. You simply do it because you love Him.

Chapter Three

Why Vertical Worship?
[Vertical Worship is posturing ourselves before the Lord]

"Ascribe to the Lord the glory of His name; bring an offering and come before Him. Worship the Lord in the splendor of [His] holiness." I Chronicles 16:29

I Chronicles 16:29 is one of the earliest scriptures that commands us to worship the Lord. We must understand that our bodies are temples of the Holy Ghost (I Corn 3:16), and that we are dead (in the flesh) in Christ, and that we have been brought at a great price. Therefore, our lives are not our own. We were created to worship the true and living God, also known as Jehovah Elohim—the only God worthy of being worshipped. Vertical Worship is reverently seeking the presence of the Lord and expressing our utter love and respect for Him without mentioning our own needs.

Many years ago, I learned the basic difference between praise and worship. When we praise God, we are giving Him thanks for what He has done for us, for delivering us out of trouble, for healing our sick bodies and for supplying all our needs. Worship talks about God to God - period. Worship tells of His attributes.

Worship esteems Him highly and says nothing about ourselves. That's why I love worship, because it takes me out of the equation. It's not about me, but it's ALL ABOUT HIM! It's when we are in this posture, this frame of mind, that we can truly give God what He wants: our adoration, our love, our devotion, and our appreciation. When our worship is vertical, it is directed straight to the Father, skipping the middleman. We are not worshipping a man, preacher, teacher, or object. We are not indirectly channeling our worship through things or another human being like so many religions do. Instead, we are going straight to the source! God is our Source, therefore He deserves all of our worship.

When I look at the Cross, I see Vertical Worship. Two pieces of wood (or any material these days) are put together, one horizontal and the other vertically. One points toward man, but the other is pointing straight up! Even with His death on the Cross, Jesus was still pointing us UPWARD!

To say that we worship God out of commandment only shows one side. We worship God out of necessity. Vertical Worship displays the love affair between the creation and the Creator.

Here are some reasons we should keep our worship vertical:

- ❖ We worship vertically because we want to display our love and affection toward the One Whom first loved us.
- ❖ We worship vertically because we want a deeper relationship with our heavenly Father.
- ❖ We worship vertically because we long to be closer to God in the perilous times.
- ❖ We worship vertically because we are madly in love with our Savior.
- ❖ We worship vertically because it gives us clarity and direction from our Savior.

Chapter Four

How do we Worship Vertically?
[Vertical Worship is a lifestyle]

"...but from there you seek the Lord your God, you shall find Him, if you look for Him with all your heart and with all your soul"
Deuteronomy 4:29

Vertical Worship is not something you put on in the morning and take off at night. Worshipping God should be the lifestyle of every believer. But often, believers do not know what to do or where to start in worshipping the Lord. Worshipping God does not always require a congregation, an organ, or a psalmist. Although they set the atmosphere for worship, we must learn how to set our own atmosphere. You can worship God anytime and anyplace. Worship must come from a place of intimacy. Below are (8) things I practice to build my personal relationship with the Lord and I pray they will help you strengthen or deepen your intimacy with the Him as well.

1) Knowing God

"That I may know Him and the power of His resurrection, and the fellowship of His sufferings, being conformed to His death."
Philippians 3:10

Knowing God is one of the most natural yearnings of the human soul, yet the enemy understands what a yielded heart to the Lord will do to his kingdom. Therefore, he tries to enter a person's life as early as possible and attempts to hinder man's natural desire to know and commune with his God. Sin separates man from God, and ever since the garden, mankind has been trying to get back into the right relationship with God. God is not hiding from us. He isn't so high that He is unobtainable. Listen to these lyrics from the song Pieces by Amanda Cook:

"Your love is a fire
It's burning bright for me
It's not a spark
It's not just a flame
Your love is a light
And all the world will see
That You don't give Your heart in pieces
And You don't hide Yourself to tease us
Your love's not fractured, it's not a troubled mind
It isn't anxious, it's not the restless kind
Your love's not passive, it's never disengaged
It's always present, it hangs on every word we say"
Your love's not broken, it's not insecure, no
Your love's not selfish, Your love is pure!
'Cause You don't give Your heart in pieces
You don't hide Yourself to tease us."

God gives us His whole heart. He wants to reveal Himself to us and, in return, wants us to reveal ourselves to Him. This is a two-way relationship. It is His desire to be in relationship with us. As a matter of fact, He wants it MORE than we do ourselves! From the beginning of time, God has made provision for the propitiation of our sin. It is His delight that we know Him. [Jeremiah 9:24] According to Jeremiah 29:13, *"You will seek Me and find Me. When you search for Me with all your heart. I will be found by you—this is the **Lord's declaration...**"*

Knowing God is essential in Vertical Worship. **YADA** is the Hebrew word for "to know." It means to know in an *intimate way*. To be intimately acquainted with one's ways. It connotes a close personal relationship, to know the innermost thoughts of another. How many of us can say that we really "know" our God? Oh yes, we know Him as Savior, Provider, Healer, and even Ruler. He is the One to whom we pray and our situations are miraculously worked out, but how many of us really KNOW HIM on an intimate level?

Francis Frangipane in His Knowing God series once said, *"to know Him is our first desire. We must know how He thinks; know His ways, what motivates Him and how He does things. He wants us to know Him no matter what we are going through. Our desire for knowing Him must remain the same. We must want Him to evade our lives and take it over..."* Now this is true YADA!

The book of Psalms is full of scriptures that echo the cries of a surrendered and yielded heart toward the Lord: *"As the deer pants for the water," "My soul follows hard after You," Teach me Your ways," "Show me Your statutes," "Conform me into Your image," "I thirst with the deepest longings to love You more."* May they also be your heart cry as you seek to know Him on a deeper intimate level.

2) Dying To Self

> *"For to me, to live is Christ, and to die is gain"*
> Philippians 1:21

"Dead Man Walking" is a term used in prison when a condemned man is walking from his prison cell to the place of execution. Someone who is about to face an unavoidable loss (though the person may not realize it). When used in this way, it is a **metaphor** comparing this loss to dying. (Wiktionary) When it comes to dying to self, I see an analogy to the dead man walking scenario. The scriptures say that before Christ came into our lives, we were dead in our trespasses and sins. Heaven was not our destination; we were on a slippery slope on our way to hell. We were that dead man, walking right into a Christless eternity. But thanks be to the Lord, we serve a forgiving and merciful God *"who turns a sinner from the error of his way ....and saves a soul from death and covers a multitude of sins."* [James 5:20] Hallelujah! But even though we have been saved from death, hell, and the grave, the scriptures still command us to *"die daily"* [I Corinthians 15:31b], and teach that *"I am dead and my life is hid with Christ in God."* [Colossians 3:3]

Dying to self is not an easy task. How do you die to the things of the world and live in the world at the same time? Living a lifestyle that is totally sold to the Lord and yet still having desires for things in the world sounds contradictory. So how can we die to self?

There is a degree of brokenness necessary to die to self. You must come to the end of yourself, realizing that nothing and no one can come between you and God—even if that other person is you. Galatians 2:20 has to become so real to you that it becomes your daily declaration: *I am crucified with Christ, nevertheless I live, yet not I, but Christ lives in me and the life which I now live in the flesh, I live by the faith of the Son of God, Who loves me and gave Himself for me."* (KJV) As I walk this Christian journey and experience the trials of life, I have to come to the stark realization that it is no longer I, but Christ. I am a dead man walking!

I am dead to the cares of this world. Dead to self-motives, selfishness, and self-exploitation. Alive to the things of Christ and all that He stands for. The challenge is that I still have natural desires. I want to be successful. I want to enjoy my family and go on vacations, but I also realize that it's so much not about me anymore, it's all about HIM!

It is the Lord's good pleasure to grant us our heart's desires. He wishes to satisfy us with long life. But it is also His will that we submerge ourselves into the things of God and be consumed by His Glory. I have concluded that if "everything I desire" does not include Him, or is not His will for my life, then I am living in vain. Philippians 3:8 speaks exactly how I feel regarding my relationship with the Lord: *"Yet indeed I also count all things loss for the excellence of the knowledge of Christ Jesus my Lord." (NKJV)* Not only do I have to know Him, but I have to die to any selfish ambitions as well. I have to move self out of the way so that God can have His way.

Dying to self takes self-sacrifice. It takes determination. It takes a "want to" attitude. It takes an "I'd rather have Jesus" mentality. It takes a longing for more of HIM and less of me. I die daily that Christ might be seen in my daily activities.

But unfortunately, some Christians think this is a bad thing. They think self-sacrifice is giving up too much of one's self. After all, God wants me happy and prosperous, doesn't He? And He does; He just wants to have chief place in your life.

So, let's try something new. Instead of thinking of ourselves and what we are currently going through, let's turn our attention to Christ and the finish work on Calvary's cross. Let our heart's cry be like that of John the Baptist, *"He must increase but I must decrease."* [John 3:30]

This is something I have not yet mastered, but the more I live, the more I realize that life isn't worth the living without Him. When I think of how fleeting life is, how people are leaving this world without time to repent, it sobers me. When I think about the time coming when I have to stand before God and give an account of my time here on earth, it makes me take inventory of what I have done for Christ. All I want Him to say is, "Well done, My good and faithful servant." Why? Because my life is not my own. I'm supposed to be dead and my life is supposed to be hid in Christ. My future life with Him is supposed to be more valuable, more precious than my life here on earth. Every day, I need to remind myself of my purpose for being here; to live a Christ-filled life, help others, pray for the world, lead people to Christ, and walk humbly before my God.

3) Practicing His Presence

> *"And He said, My Presence will go with you, and I will give you rest."*
> Exodus 33:14

According to Jeremiah 23:23, *"Am I a God near at hand,"* says the Lord, *And not a God afar off?"* This is what the Lord says about Himself. He is not a distant God; He is only a breath away. God is OMNIPRESENT. He is everywhere, all at the same time. We as humans often forget this major attribute of God. However, we as believers need to have a greater awareness of His presence. We need to set aside some time, block out the rest of the world and concentrate on Him. How many of us take time and sit in His presence with absolutely nothing to say? How many of us enter into His presence with a broken and contrite spirit? When was the last time you sat, knelt, or laid before Him and were overwhelmed by His very presence?

Unfortunately, because of the cares of this world, very little time is given to sit before our God. Most of us have such hectic lifestyles, myself included, that we don't have time to maintain relationships with others, much less with God. This is a sad statement, but true. We as humans have displaced our loyalty, focus, and passion for the true and living God and gotten off course. What I am suggesting is that we go back to our First Love. We must cultivate our relationship with the Lord, because to be honest with you, it is the only relationship that really matters in the scheme of things. Nothing else will work. Nothing else will line up.

We cannot allow the cares of this world to choke God out. We need Him. We need His Presence. In His presence, there is fullness of joy. In His presence there is peace. We must become more protective of the Presence of God. We must guard it with our very lives.

In Psalms 51, King David was so fearful that the Lord was going to lift His hand off his life after committing sin with Bathsheba and having her husband killed, that he cried out, *"Do not cast me away from Your presence, and do not take Your Holy Spirit from me."* Psalms 51:11 (NKJV) Man, that is the worst place in the world to be! Can you imagine God withdrawing Himself from your life? I couldn't! I would be most miserable. Life is hard enough battling demonic forces and staying in my right mind with God in my life. I cannot imagine life without Him. David learned a valuable lesson. He knew that even though he was King, a life without the presence of God was no life at all.

Unfortunately, even though our God is omnipresent, it doesn't mean that we have access to His presence. According to Psalm 101:7, *"He who works deceit shall not dwell within My house; He who tells lies shall not continue in My presence."* Therefore, we cannot take God's presence for granted.

God's Presence is one of the most necessary elements we can experience in our Christian lives. It is essential to a healthy and growing relationship with Him. His Presence is so calming, so reassuring. In His Presence there is joy, peace, and pleasures forevermore.

Here are a few tips you can use to practice His Presence:

1. **Tell the Lord you love Him the moment you wake up**: before you even get out of bed.
2. **Talk to the Lord as you are getting ready**: Include Him in the minute details of your day.
3. **Listen to anointed worship music**: music that speaks well of Him, His attributes, and His beauty. Let it create an atmosphere that will help you enter His Presence.
4. **Praise God for His goodness**: praise Him for His goodness toward you. Think of how He woke you up in your right mind or how He has protected you from the enemy. How He made a way out of no way.
5. **Worship God for His character**: we as believers sometimes forget what an awesome God we serve. Here are a few of His characteristics that we can meditate on as we worship Him:

    He is Omniscience—all-knowing
    He is Omnipotent—all-powerful
    He is Omnipresent—everywhere at the same time

He is Omnibenevolent—supremely good
He is Immutable—unchanging and unable to be changed
He's Eternal—He always was and always will be
Speak of His beauty, wisdom, and greatness.

6. **Meditate on the Word of God:** with today's technology, there are so many ways to get the Word of God into your spirit. We are without excuses! We have the Word on CD, Internet, iPad, Kindle, cell phone, and there is always the good old-fashioned way—reading the bible in written form. The Word of God is sharper than any two-sided sword. The Word brings us comfort, reassurance, and confidence.

7. **Sit in total silence with a heart focused on Him:** this is the easiest yet hardest thing to do. It costs nothing, you can do it anywhere, and it doesn't require any else except a willing heart.

Psalms 16:11 shares with us one of the most important results of practicing the presence of God, "You will show me the path of life; In Your presence is fullness of joy; At Your right hand are pleasures forevermore." We can experience great joy in the presence of the Lord. We just have to take the time and do it.

It is in God's presence where the eyes of our understanding are enlightened [Eph.1:18]. God uses the minister, pastor, and or teacher to share this knowledge, but most of our walk with Him is going to be a one-on-one experience, which requires spending quality time with Him. God is longing to share His deep revelations with us, but we must pay the price and make the sacrifice of spending time with Him.

The funny thing about it is that it really shouldn't be a sacrifice—and there is no price large enough to pay that can come remotely close to the benefit of spending time with Him. He is the almighty, omniscience, omnipresent and omnipotent God. Who, when given the opportunity, wouldn't want to spend time with Him? Why do we as humans find it such a chore to go into the presence of our Heavenly Father? Our Maker? Our Redeemer? Don't we owe Him that much respect? Isn't He worth the minutes or hours of the day that we spend with Him? If we think the One who gave us breath is not worth taking the time out of our busy schedule to sit with or talk to, then either we have been blinded by the enemy or we have lost our righteous minds. Just think about it. We can spend countless hours sitting before the TV watching movies, sitcoms, sporting events or soap operas, but it is inconvenient to spend time with the God of the universe. Or life happens and we slowly push our time with God out of our daily routine.

If we value our relationship with the Lord like we value our relationships with our loved ones, if we spend time with Him like we do with our favorite pastime, sport or hobby, where would we be? Our lives will be so much richer, fuller, and more satisfying. We would experience a peace that cannot be found in this world as we know it.

God's presence strengthens and fortifies us. Incorporate Him into your daily lifestyle. Treat Him like the best friend you never had. Act like He is present in your daily living. Talk to Him often. Act like He is present all day, every day. After all, He is ever-present. He's just waiting on us to realize it.

There is nothing on earth which can compare to His Presence. Absolutely nothing.

4) Acknowledging His Deity

> *"I am the Lord, and there is no other. There is no God besides Me."*
> Isaiah 45:5

We as born-again believers have the honor and privilege to worship the God of the Universe. This is another truth that we as human beings haven't truly comprehended. In his message about Christ and the cross, Dr. Tony Evans once said, *"Saints don't appreciate the cross, otherwise we would live differently."* I thought this was so profound and spoke volumes about how we as Christians are living today. We are so consumed with our own issues, so self-absorbed with the cares of this world, that we often forget who God really is. He is the all sufficient, all consuming, all wise GOD. Deuteronomy 6:4 declares it good and loud: *"Hear, O Israel: The LORD our God is one LORD."* Hallelujah, Jehovah Elohim!

One good way to acknowledge His deity is to rehearse the various aspects of His character. When you read the Old Testament, it is full of accounts where God showed His people different aspects of Himself.

There are also plenty of books out there that describe the attributes of God in great detail. Knowing and understanding who He really is and how awesome He is will help you acknowledge His Deity. One good book that speaks about the different names of Gods is "Praying the Names of God" by Ann Spangler. This book will give you an excellent overview of what the Names of God mean and then show you how to use them in your personal prayer time with Him.

Below are just a few of our God's names that display His magnificent characteristics:

- Elohim (God) (Genesis 1:1)
- El Shaddai (Lord God Almighty) (Genesis 17:1-2)
- El Elyon (The Most High God) (Daniel 4:34)
- El Roi (The God Who sees me) (Genesis 16:13-14)
- Adonai (Lord, Master) (Psalm 16:2)
- Yahweh (Lord, Jehovah) (Exodus 3:14-15)
- Jehovah Nissi (The Lord My Banner) (Exodus 17:15)
- Jehovah-Raah (The Lord My Shepherd) (Psalms 23:1)
- Jehovah Rapha (The Lord That Heals) (Exodus 15:26)
- Jehovah Shammah (The Lord Is There) (Ezekiel 48:35)
- Jehovah Tsidkenu (The Lord Our Righteousness) (Jer.23:6)
- Jehovah Shalom (The Lord Is Peace) (Judges 6:24)

So let us acknowledge His Deity and give Him the honor due His name. God always responds when His children call Him by His redemptive name(s).

5) Tell Him you love Him often

"And thou shall love the Lord thy God with all thy heart and with all thy soul and with all thy mind and with all thy strength—this is the first commandment."
Mark 12:30

Make Him the Object of your affection!

Remember when you were first fell in love with the love of your life? Remember how you stayed up nights talking on the phone, no one wanting to be the first one to hang up. They were the last person you thought of before you went to sleep and the first one you thought of when you woke up the next day. Remember how you would write each other love letters declaring your undying love? You wanted to please them with your gifts, and you paid close attention to the things that would bring them joy. There's nothing like the feeling when you are in love. There is a feeling of excitement, anticipation, and pure joy just to be in the other's presence. It's an indescribable feeling that makes you never want to be apart.

Well, that's the way I feel about the Lord. I get excited about our meeting times. I wait with expectation just to be in His presence again. I wake up whispering, "I love You, Lord." I seek Him out and am concerned about the things that concern Him. And I am saddened about the things that hurt His heart.

Like any relationship, it takes work to keep the love fresh and alive, and if I am to be fully transparent, I drop the ball sometimes and am not as passionate about the Lord as I should be. But because of the indwelling of the Holy Spirit, He gently guides me back on track and I run back to Him with apologies for my slackness, and we continue with our loving relationship.

The Lord has made us the object of His affection since the beginning of time—so why don't we make Him the object of ours? He loves it when we love on Him. I don't know about you, but it makes me feel good when people express their love for me. Simple gestures like a phone call, a card in the mail, or a bouquet of flowers let a person know you are thinking about them and that you care. We serve a God who feels. He delights, He rejoices, He sings, He angers, He loves, and He wants to hear from **you**! From your lips to God's ears, He wants to hear how much He really means to you. How do you lavish your love on Him? Start by pursuing Him. Hungering for Him. Panting after Him. Write the Lord a love letter, pouring out your heart. Share your innermost secrets with Him, knowing that He will still accept you, warts and all. Let Him know that no one will ever take His place and that He has the number one place in your heart.

Lavishing your love on the Lord is telling Him how much you love Him. This is best illustrated by the song "I Love You Lord" by Laurie Adams-Klein:

I love You Lord
And I lift my voice
To worship You
Oh, my soul rejoices!
Take joy my King
In what You hear
Let it be a sweet, sweet sound in Your ear.
1978 by House of Mercy Music.

6) Develop a lasting friendship with Him

"Abraham believed God, and it was counted to him as righteousness"—and he was called a friend of God." James 2:23

Do you remember having a best friend when you were growing up? That was the person whom you hung out with the most. Your ride or die person. You played together, shared triumphs and heartbreaks. You ate at each other's homes, shared secrets and cried together. Their parents accepted you as a part of the family. You were inseparable.

Proverbs 18:24 says, "there is a friend that sticketh closer than a brother." Jesus can be that best friend, but you have to let Him in. We have to learn not only to cultivate a love relationship, but also how to cultivate a friendship with God. Like any relationship, it starts with trust. The more you trust someone, the more you will open up to them. Trust God with your secrets. Tell Him how you "really" feel, no sugar coating. Express the desires of your heart to Him. Express your failures and shortcomings, your disappointments and accomplishments. Share it all with Him. And check this out—because of His omniscience, you can be real with Him, withholding nothing, because He knows it all anyway. He just loves it when we come to Him and share our hearts. How awesome is that to have a best friend who knows everything?

Spending time with the Lord will develop that friendship. Realizing that He is on your side and only wants the best for you will help you open up to Him and be vulnerable. Even when you are wrong, tell Him. When you are mad, tell Him. When you are on the verge of giving up, tell Him. He is nigh unto them that are of a broken spirit and contrite heart. (Psalm 51:27)

Best friends do not always have to speak when they are in each other's presence. There is an understanding between the two that just being in the room with each other is enough. I can be alone with God and not utter a word. Just being with Him is enough for me. Sharing quiet times with Him is the best.

The Lord is a keeper of secrets. You can share your deepest, darkest secrets with Him without fear of them being repeated.

God hears you. God sees you and God cares for you. He is concerned about your every need, so let Him in so He can do what He does best: love on you.

7) Sing love songs to Him

"I will be glad and rejoice in thee: I will sing praise to thy name, O thou most High."
Psalms 9:29

There are thousands upon thousands of love songs out there written specifically to the Lord by anointed songwriters who have put down their feelings toward the Lord on paper and have set them to music. They have invited us to come along to worship and adore the God of our Salvation.

The key to selecting a song to sing to Him is the lyrics. Always check out the words to the song and what are they saying. Are they lifting Him up or acknowledging His Lordship? Are they pointing you toward the Lord and not yourself? Are they speaking of His magnificent beauty and splendor? These are the lyrics you would want to sing to the Lord. If you ever find yourself at a loss for words in worshipping God, put on a worship song and if the lyrics come into agreement with how you feel about the Lord, sing them directly to the Lord as if you wrote them yourself.

There is one song that I love to sing to the Lord when I want to remind Him of what He really means to me:

When I look into Your holiness

When I look into Your holiness
When I gaze into Your loveliness
When all things that surround become shadows
In the light of You

When I've found the joy of reaching Your heart
When my will become enthroned in Your love
When all things that surround become shadows
In the light of You

I worship You I worship You
The reason I live is to worship You
I worship You I worship You
The reason I live is to worship You
Wayne & Cathy Perrin © 1981 Integrity's Hosanna! Music

Singing to the Lord takes you away from what's going on around you and helps you be singularly focused on the Lord.

Zephaniah 3:17 says, *"The Lord thy **God in** the midst of thee is mighty; He will save, He will rejoice **over** thee with joy; He will rest **in** His love, He will joy **over** thee with **singing**."* He loves singing too and He sings over us. Wouldn't it be awesome if we flipped the script and sing over Him? He is so worthy of every ounce of words we can give Him whether it's via spoken words or singing words to Him.

I'll pour my love on you

[Chorus]
Like oil upon Your feet
Like wine for You to drink
Like water from my heart
I pour my love on You
If praise is like perfume
I'll lavish mine on You
Till every drop is gone
I'll pour my love on You
(Copyright © 2002-2010 All The Lyrics .com)

8) Acknowledge Personage of the Holy Spirit

"Do you not know that you are the temple of God and that the Spirit of God dwells in you?" I Corinthians 3:16

The Holy Spirit has often been the most neglected person of the Holy Trinity. We praise God, sing love songs to Jesus, and the Holy Spirit sometimes receives an honorable mention.

The Greek word *Paraclete* translates to "Comforter" or "Counselor." He comes alongside those who call on Him and brings guidance and direction to our lives. The Holy Spirit is mentioned over a hundred times in the bible. Therefore, He should be acknowledged.

Psalm 139 speaks a lot about God's Omnipresence and lets us know that we are never alone:
"Where can I go from Your Spirit?
Where can I flee from Your presence?
If I go up to the heavens, You are there;
If I make my bed in the depths, You are there.
If I rise on the wings of the dawn,
If I settle on the far side of the sea,
even there Your hand will guide me,
Your right hand will hold me fast."

These are some things that I have experienced by having the Holy Spirit operating in my life:
- ❖ He has become my Confidant
- ❖ He has been my Revealer of Truth
- ❖ He has convicted me of my sin
- ❖ He constantly brings scripture back to my memory
- ❖ He guides me through the day

According to Wikipedia, the seven gifts of the Holy Spirit are **wisdom, understanding, counsel, fortitude, knowledge, piety, and fear of the Lord.**

Over the years, I have developed such a love and dependency on the Holy Spirit. And like Benny Hinn, in his book "Good Morning Holy Spirit," I say good morning to the Holy Spirit when I wake up every day.

I can testify to the scriptures when John 14:26 says, "But the Advocate, the Holy Spirit, whom the Father will send in My name, will teach you all things and will remind you of everything I have said to you." The Holy Spirit brings back things to my remembrance all the time.

In his article, "Thirteen Characteristics of The Holy Spirit," John Van Gelderen lists some major characteristics we all should know. Here are just a few:

1. He is the Spirit of truth
2. He is the Spirit of holiness
3. He is the Spirit of life in Christ
4. He is the Spirit of faith
5. He is the Spirit of wisdom
6. He is the Spirit of revelation in the knowledge of God
7. He is the Spirit of a sound mind

Indeed, the Holy Spirit is all that and so much more. The Holy Spirit is my inner strength. I rely on Him every day. Not a day goes by when I don't receive clear direction from Him regarding some of the simplest tasks, like which way I should drive to work or remembering my bank card, and the important things such as giving me directions to write this book.

I encourage you to incorporate the Holy Spirit into your daily life. Get to know Him and allow Him to orchestrate the affairs of your life. He will enhance your life and bring clarity to those things you are unsure of. I promise you, He will never steer you wrong.

Chapter Five

The Benefits of Vertical Worship
[Vertical Worship is entering a realm of intimacy with the Lord]

"But from there you will seek the LORD your God, and you will find Him if you seek Him with all your heart and with all your soul." Deuteronomy 4:29

There are many benefits to Vertical Worship. Shifting your worship from people and things to the King of Kings is the greatest benefit of all. Here are some other benefits that come when you purposely choose to direct your focus upward to the Lord.

God wants to have a relationship with us. He has done everything within His power to not only **establish** this relationship, but also a way to **maintain** this relationship. He knows we are mere flesh and that the flesh will fail us often, so He designed a remedy called repentance which allows us to enter back into this covenant, should we step out of it due to temporary insanity! The Lord wants us to worship Him. It is out of our devoted love and appreciation for the finished work of Calvary that He wants us to FREELY give Him our hearts. When we die to self and submit ourselves to God, we can totally submerge ourselves in God's purposes and His plans for our lives.

God has and always will uphold His side of the covenant, but after realizing that mankind could not live up to our end of the bargain, God sent His Son Jesus to fulfill our side of the covenant. Hallelujah! If we accept Him as our personal Lord and Savior, we all have a right to the Tree of Life. We all have a right to God's promises kept in His covenant. If that is not worth worshipping God, then I don't know what is!

Learning to set our affections on things above is not an easy task, but it is obtainable. You may be already using some of the principles I mentioned earlier in this book. Maybe you just needed a jumpstart to get you going again, or maybe you are brand new to this level of thinking. Whichever stage you're in, it's never too late to begin.

There are definite benefits to Vertical Worship:

- We can come into agreement with God and not struggle with Him concerning His will for our lives.
- We can truly minister to God's people from the heart of God.
- We can operate under a greater anointing for ministry.
- We can truly flow in the gifts of God that are on our lives—without perverting or prostituting the gift.
- We can live in the genuine peace of God that passes all understanding.
- We can experience the joy of the Lord which is our strength.
- We can enter into His rest, knowing that He is in control.
- We can experience a deeper, closer walk with the Lord as we gain a stronger sense of who He really is.

The bottom line is, the more you worship Him, the more you grow in love, wisdom, grace and power.

Chapter Six

The Vertical Worshipper
[Vertical Worship is blocking out the world and losing yourself in His presence]

"You will show me the path of life; In Your presence is fullness of joy; At Your right hand are pleasures forevermore."
Psalms 16:11

I was once told by a very dear friend that, *"Vertical Worship Creative Arts Ministries will only be birthed out of Vertical Worship."* This statement is very true. I cannot expect to do any great exploits for God without <u>first</u> engaging in Vertical Worship myself.

How can I lead people where I've never been? How can I talk about how we should worship God and make Him number one in our lives if I never make Him number one in my own life? How can I tell you to *'keep it vertical,"* if I'm not the first partaker? In other words, I must practice what I preach. In this busy lifestyle of ours, it is easy to let our EGO (Easing God Out) get in the way, but we must fight this internal battle and not allow our egos to impede our pursuit of an intimate relationship with God.

What kind of worshipper is the Lord looking for? One who is truthful, honest, and reliable. One who will worship out of a genuine relationship and not out of emotions. It is true that during the worship experience, we will experience various emotions because our emotions are engaged. God doesn't want a lifeless worshipper. But at the same time, your worship should not be based on emotion alone. The Lord is looking for one who is totally surrendered and committed to Him and His righteous cause.

I Corinthians 3:16 says, *"When one turns to the Lord, the veil is taken away."* This is such a powerful scripture. Jesus often spoke in parables to get His message across. He often used the foolish things to confound the wise. There is a veil over the eyes of those who do not know the Lord. They are not sensitive to the things of God; neither do they see the need to know God. However, there can also be a veil over the eyes of a believer. In our Christian lives, there will be times when we do not see things clearly. We may need a solution to a difficult situation. This is when we need to turn to the Lord and allow Him to take the veil away, take the confusion away, take the blindness away, and give us a solution and insight into what we are going through.

Sometimes we need the Lord to give us clarity to a particular scripture. As we read it and ponder over God's Word, as we turn our faces toward Him, He will remove the veil and give us a clearer understanding of His Word.

My Paradigm Shift

Years ago, I experienced something strange. It wasn't depression, neither was it low self-esteem or doubt. It went much deeper than that. Bishop T.D. Jakes, in his message entitled, "The Weight of Glory," called it a *nonsensical pain*. An inner pain or dull ache that just does not make sense, because there is nothing terribly wrong with the way your life is going. I came to a point in my life when I realized I was carrying around a weight of Glory that the Lord had put on me. It was the strangest weight that I have ever experienced. It was a lonely place, but I felt a deep sense of peace with God. It was a defining moment. It was my **paradigm shift**—a change of mind from the status quo. I had finally reached a point in my life that either I would go all the way with God, partner with Him and allow Him to have complete control of my life, or I would not. Either I would step all the way over from being a surface worshipper to having a deeper, richer intimacy with the Father that I have never experienced before, or I would not. Either I would believe what He said about me and walk in the power of His Word, or I would not. Man, I tell you, God really knows how to get you to come to the end of yourself. This was my defining moment and by the grace of God, I rose to the occasion and said, "Yes, I choose You, Lord."

My relationship with Christ is the most important thing in my life. I must nurture it. I must protect it. I must value it. Without it, I would be miserable. I have realized it wouldn't matter if I had a million dollars in the bank, a loving spouse, a beautiful home with obedient children, and the car of my dreams. None of these material things can make me genuinely happy. Oh, they can ease the pressure of life. They can bring a degree of happiness to my life, but they cannot give me the intrinsic joy that only comes through knowing Christ. And the only way to go deeper with the

Lord is to redirect my focus vertically toward Him. It's only when I realign my desires to hunger and thirst after HIM and be totally consumed by HIM that I will find satisfaction in all the other things—the house, the car, the relationships, etc. Therefore, I no longer pray so much for the "things" because I know if I had them, I would still not be satisfied. I now pray for more of HIM, so I can enjoy those things when they come into my life.

Living for the Well Done

"His Lord said to him, 'Well done, good and faithful servant; you have been faithful over a few things, I will make you ruler over many things. Enter into the joy of your Lord.'" Matthew 25:23

I have been around the church for a long time. I have experienced a few major dominations and have seen a lot of things. One thing I have observed in the Body of Christ is that we like to entertain each other. We can out-preach, out-sing and out-dance each other, but at the end of the day, what have we accomplished? What are our eternal results? I've heard this saying all my saved life: *"Only what you do for Christ will last."* The older I get, the more this statement has become a reality to me. There is a scripture that rings true in my heart: *"well done good and faithful servant."* [Matt. 25:23a] This scripture is taken from the parable of the five talents, but we can also apply it to our personal relationship with the Lord.

The more I live, the more I realize that a lot of what I do is just spiritual gymnastics. I have done a lot of things in the Kingdom, but have I been effective? Have I made an impact? Have I followed the pattern the Lord has laid out for my life? More importantly, have I done what the Lord asked me to do? Very simple questions, but the answers are often laced with excuses, reasons, and rationales...all leading up to an unfortunate "no." Often, the excuses sound a little like these: "I would have, but..." "I couldn't because..." "I was going to..." "I didn't have the resources." "I don't have the help." The list goes on and on.

When I look at the condition of the world we are currently living in and see a people whose hearts are so far away from the Lord, it saddens me. When I see that people do not love Jesus, do not want Jesus, or don't even want to know Jesus, it makes me more determined to be an example and live a Christ-centered life. I am more determined to do what He wants me to do. That old saying from my past now rings true in my own life: **ONLY WHAT I DO FOR CHRIST IS GOING TO LAST!** Only doing what He has required from me is going to matter. I can do 101 things right, but if I don't do that one thing He has <u>designed</u> me to do, what He has <u>called</u> me to do, what He has <u>asked</u> me to do, then all that I have done would have been in vain.

When I stand before my God, when He asks me whether I did what He asked me to do, He doesn't want to hear, "I couldn't because I was offended." "I couldn't because I didn't have time." "I didn't because I was afraid." "I didn't because I was mad at You." No. When I stand before God, I want to hear, *"Well done, good and faithful servant."* **I AM LIVING FOR THE WELL DONE.** The sum total of my existence is that I pleased my God.

Erma Bombeck said it best when she wrote the following statement: *"When I stand before God at the end of my life, I would hope that I would not have a single bit of talent left, and could say, 'I used everything You gave me."* Oh God, how this quote gets to me! At the end of the day, I want to be empty.

Empty of all the dreams.
Empty of all the books.
Empty of all the conferences.
Empty of all the inventions that He has given me to birth into the earthly realm. I must be about my Father's business, but the only way I am going to be successful is to stay in His Face, to dwell in His presence and align myself with Him vertically so that I can carry out all that He has purposed my heart to do.

Chapter Seven

The Heart Cry of Vertical Worship
[Vertical Worship is being consumed by God]

"My soul is crushed with longing after Your ordinances at all times." Psalm 119:20

As I stated at the beginning of this book, before we can effectively minister to the world horizontally, we must first be aligned with the Lord vertically. This is the heart cry of Vertical Worship.

We are living in a world with little or no regard for God. The only Christ most of them will ever see is Christ in us. However, if we don't represent Christ in a positive and effective way, we won't give the world anything to ascribe to.

Matthew 5:13 states: *""You are the salt of the earth; but if the salt loses its flavor, how shall it be seasoned? It is then good for nothing but to be thrown out and trampled underfoot by men."* (NKJV) How can we ignite the world without fire, how can we have fire without passion, and how can we have passion without a real love relationship with God? Matthew 5:16 goes on to show us our responsibility in winning the lost: *"Let your light so shine before men, that they may see your good works and glorify your Father in heaven."* (NKJV)

Until the Body of Christ, the church (Ecclesia), and the called out ones boldly proclaim their love, devotion and adoration for Jesus Christ, the world will continue to go to hell in a handbasket. Our bar is too low. We must set the standard as the church of the only true and living God. The world needs to see our passion for our God in order to whet their appetites and raise their curiosity about this God that we serve. They should come to us inquiring about our joy during difficult times or our peace during calamity. And when they come to us, we can share with them the reason for our joy and peace—His name is Jesus Christ.

Chapter Eight

My Worship Is Vertical!
[Vertical Worship is a conviction]

Looking unto Jesus the author and finisher of our faith; Who for the joy that was set before Him endured the cross, despising the shame, and is set down at the right hand of the throne of God.
Hebrews 12:2

We are spirit, and we worship God in Spirit and in truth. The flesh blocks our spirits from having a real relationship with God. We must reach a point where we allow nothing, not even our flesh, to impede our relationship with the Lord. This is why a lifestyle of fasting and prayer needs to be established in every believer's life.

Overall, my journey with the Lord has been a good one. There have been many bumps in the road and disappointments (more in myself than God), but there have also been triumphs and victories, and as my grandmother would say, "I won't give nothing for my journey." Why? Because it was necessary. I had to go through trials so I would have first-hand knowledge of who God is and what He can do. I am so glad that He introduced me to worship early in my walk with Him, because it shaped my life. It was worship that saved my life. It was worship that drew me closer to Him.

In the good times, I look vertically to Him. In the bad times, I look vertically to Him. And in my dry seasons, I look vertically to Him. I can indeed proclaim that my worship is Vertical.

A Word on Fasting

When it comes to fasting, no one says it better than Jentezen Franklin. I love his definition of fasting: *"Simply stated, biblical fasting is refraining from food for a spiritual purpose."*

When we fast, we are saying to our flesh, "I will not give into your desires right now because I want my spirit man to become a little more sensitive to what God is saying." In our quest to know God better and become more intimate with Him, there will be times when we need to turn our plates down and be alone with God.

Desperate times call for desperate measures, and the bottom-line is how desperate are you? How close do you want to get to God? How much do you value hearing His voice? How intimate do you want to become with Him? The bible says in James 8:4, *"Draw near to God and He will draw near to you."* And He will. He honors our self-sacrificing behavior, no matter how small the sacrifice. We are letting Him know that He is more important to us than whatever is going on right now.

I encourage you to develop a life of fasting. Pick a day out of the week and dedicate it to the Lord. Set aside some special time for Him and say, "This is Your day. This is Your time." There are different types of fasts to choose from. Seek the Lord and let Him guide you.

Here are a few:

1) Absolute Fast: give up all food except liquids.
2) Partial Fast: give up food for a specific timeframe.
3) Daniel Fast: give up delicacies like sweets, soda, meats, and breads. It is basically fruits and vegetables (there are a few variations on this fast).

To learn more about fasting, visit Jentzen Franklin's website or read his book on fasting. They are both excellent resources.

Chapter Nine

My Declarations
[Vertical Worship is a mindset]

*"Great is **the LORD**, and greatly to be **praised**; and His greatness is unsearchable" Psalms 145:3*

One day, after sitting before the Lord, I sensed a powerful pull in my Spirit regarding my purpose in life. I was having another defining moment. It was not deep. It was not spectacular. But it was a deliberate act to totally surrender to Him and all that comes with that act of surrender. I suddenly had a keen awareness of what the Christian life was all about and what it means to give Him preeminence in my own life. I think we make this Christian walk more difficult than it really is. God wants our hearts, but it seems to be the hardest part of ourselves to give. Funny, but it's when the Lord requires more of us that we realize how much "alive" to self we really are.

What I love about the Lord is that He knows the innermost workings of our hearts. No matter how much we kick and scream against giving Him our all, He keeps working with us, allowing various situations to arise, allowing difficult relationships to exist until we come to a point of total surrender. It was after this encounter with Christ that I wrote the following declaration to the Lord.

Our God is:
- Unshakeable
- Unrelentless
- Unending
- Unfailing
- Unbeatable
- Unrivaled
- Unmovable
- Unreserved
- Unrestrained
- Uncontrolled
- Uncontained
- And Incomparable

In Summary

[Vertical Worship is an internal yearning]

Vertical Worship can be expressed in different ways by different people.

Vertical Worship is **PURE**.
Vertical Worship is **INTIMATE.**
Vertical Worship is **INTENTIONAL**
Vertical Worship is **SEEKING HIM OUT.**

Proclaim your vertical worship every day by directing your thoughts and life upward. Acknowledge His Deity and sing Him love songs. Develop a genuine friendship with God and spend time alone with Him. Respect the personage of the Holy Spirit and include Him in your daily life. Love on God and hold Him close to your heart. Get to know your God—I promise you it will take you a lifetime. And last, die to self and allow the Christ in you to have preeminence in your life.

Be passionate about God and the things of God. Do not take your relationship with God for granted. It is an honor and privilege to be in relationship with the Omniscient, Omnipotent, and Omnipresent God.

Do not allow anything or anybody to get in between you and your God. I know you have heard this saying over and over again, but it bears repeating: "We are the only Jesus most people are going to see." We must represent Him correctly. It is crucial for two reasons:

1) We have to stand before God and give an account.
2) Our lifestyle can lead others to Christ.

The Surrendered Life

By Angela D. Brown

God wants all of me.
God wants a surrendered heart.
God wants a surrendered mind.
Gods wants a surrendered will.
God wants a surrendered thought life.
God wants entrance into every nook and cranny of our lives
so that we can boldly declare:
ALL I HAVE IS YOURS LORD!

He longs to have an intimate fellowship with His creation.
Whether we dialog with Him or sit in complete silence.
He desires an oneness with us.
There is nothing we can say, reveal or confess that.
He does not already know.
He searches the hearts of men and He knows the
inner working of our minds.
He sits and He waits until we come into agreement with His Word,
for we can do nothing without Him.
We need Him.
We need His Direction.
We need His Love.
We need His Chastisement.
We need His Favor.
We need His Provision.
We need His Deliverance.
We need His Salvation.
We need His Protection.
We need You Lord – Oh, how we need You!
Don't let our pompous exterior fool You.
We are utterly dependent on You.
We need You.
ALL OF YOU!

BIBLIOGRAPHY

Wycliffe's Bible Encyclopedia

Pieces by Amanda Cook:
Songwriters: Steffany Dawn Gretzinger / Amanda Lindsey Cook.
Bethel Music Publishing

Excerpts from Dr.Tony Evans sermon

"Praying the Names of God" by Ann Spangler

Names of God - http://www.blueletterbible.org

"Good Morning Holy Spirit" by Benny Hinn

"I Love You Lord" by Laurie Adams-Klein
1978 by House of Mercy Music.

"When I look into Your holiness" by Wayne & Cathy Perrin
© 1981 Integrity's Hosanna! Music

"I'll pour my love on You" by Philips, Craig & Dean
(Copyright © 2002-2010 All The Lyrics .com)

Wikipedia

Thirteen Characteristics of The Holy Spirit", by John Van Gelderen.
Posted Oct 31, 2018 | Holy Spirit | 2
https://www.revivalfocus.org/thirteen-characteristics-holy-spirit/

Excerpts from Bishop T.D. Jakes, "The Weight of Glory" sermon

"Fasting" by Jentezen Franklin

www.ingramcontent.com/pod-product-compliance
Lightning Source LLC
Chambersburg PA
CBHW050448010526